USING A SPREADSHEET TO TALLY

YOUR FINANCES

PROPER FINANCER ORGANIZATION WITH

SPREADSHEET

KATE .P

Table of Contents

CHAPTER ONE

INTRODUCTION

Achieving long-term goals and financial stability need effective personal money management. Spreadsheets are a useful tool for recording and managing finances. Spreadsheets are useful for tracking spending, creating budgets, and keeping tabs on financial success because they provide flexibility, customization, and organization. We'll look at using a spreadsheet to efficiently manage your finances in this guide. This tutorial will provide you useful advice on how to make the most of spreadsheets for improved financial management, regardless of whether you're new to budgeting or want to simplify your current method. Let's get started and use a spreadsheet to help you take charge of your money.

The significance of organizing and tracking finances

Organization and tracking of finances are crucial for a number of reasons:

Consciousness of Spending: Keeping tabs on your money lets you know where it's going. It gives you insights into your spending patterns and makes it easier for you to see where you could be overspending and where you might be able to save costs.

Budgeting: The basis of any budget is keeping track of your financial situation. You can make a budget that fits your priorities and financial goals

5

by keeping track of your income and expenses. A budget aids in responsible money allocation, future expense planning, and preventive spending.

Setting Financial Goals: By keeping your finances organized, you may monitor and establish goals for yourself. A comprehensive understanding of your financial status enables you to set reasonable goals and track your advancement over time, regardless of the reason for your savings a trip, a down payment on a house, or retirement.

Debt management: Keeping track of your finances will help you handle debt better. You can create a plan to pay off debt strategically, give priority to paying off high-interest debt, and prevent taking on more debt by keeping track of your payments and debts.

Emergency Preparedness: Having your money in order gives you wiggle room in case of an emergency. You can be better prepared to meet unforeseen financial obstacles, such medical expenditures or auto repairs, without getting into debt by keeping an emergency fund and keeping track of your spending.

Tax Preparation: Accurate and simpler tax preparation results from keeping thorough financial records. Keeping track of invoices, receipts, and other financial records throughout the year can help you optimize credits and deductions and expedite the tax filing process.

Financial Security: Keeping tabs on and managing your money is a good way to feel secure and at ease financially generally. You might feel more confident in your capacity to overcome financial obstacles and accomplish your long-term objectives when you are aware of your financial situation and have a strategy in place.

Financial Awareness: Keeping a regular record of your finances helps you become more thoughtful and financially aware. It motivates you to make wise financial decisions that are consistent with your beliefs and objectives, to be more aware of your spending patterns, and to give needs precedence over wants.

In general, attaining financial stability, accomplishing your financial objectives, and keeping control over your finances all depend on keeping track of and organizing your finances. You may make wiser financial decisions, feel less stressed, and lay a strong basis for a stable financial future by maintaining organization and knowledge.

Organizing Your Spreadsheet

Creating a spreadsheet to track your finances is a simple process that you can tailor to your own requirements and tastes. This is how to begin:

Pick a Spreadsheet Program: Go for a program that you feel at ease with. Apple Numbers, Google Sheets, and Microsoft Excel are popular choices. Select the program that best suits your needs and accessibility from those that offer comparable features and functionality.

Make a New Spreadsheet: Launch the spreadsheet application of your choice, then start a fresh, empty spreadsheet. Your financial monitoring system will begin as a clean slate for you to create and modify.

Create Columns and Rows: To efficiently arrange your financial data, create columns and rows. Typical columns could be:

Date: Make a note of the day of every transaction.

Give a brief description of the transaction, such as groceries, utilities, or eating out.

Sort each transaction into a category (such as lodging, travel, or entertainment).

Amount: Keep track of the total amount spent on each transaction.

Declare if each transaction is an expense or a revenue source.

Prepare the Spreadsheet: Organize your data so that it is both aesthetically pleasing and simple to read. Adapt fonts, colors, and cell borders to improve organization and readability. When highlighting headings or crucial information, think about utilizing bold font or shading.

Configure formulae and Functions: To automate computations and expedite data entry, utilize formulae and functions. As an illustration:

Determine the overall revenue and expenses for every category using the sum function.

Auto-fill: To populate formulas or recurring transactions across several rows, use auto-fill.

Conditional formatting: Use conditional formatting to draw attention to transactions that fit certain requirements (such as spending more than a predetermined amount).

Add More Sheets or Tabs: If you want to arrange different areas of your money, think about adding more sheets or tabs to your spreadsheet. You might, for instance, have different sheets for financial summaries, savings targets, budgeting, and cost tracking.

Add Summary Sections: To give a summary of your financial situation and advancement toward your objectives, create summary sections or tables. Provide a summary of important data including overall income, overall spending, savings rate, and progress made toward savings objectives.

Update and Review Frequently: Make a commitment to updating and evaluating your spreadsheet on a frequent basis to make sure it is accurate and pertinent. Allocate a specific period of time every week or month to enter new transactions, balance accounts, and assess your financial advancement.

Spreadsheet Backup: In order to guard against data loss, it's critical to often create spreadsheet backups. To make sure your financial data is safe, think about backing it up to an external hard drive or cloud storage service.

Personalize to Your Preferences: Tailor your spreadsheet to your own tastes and financial objectives. Try out various features, formulas, and layouts to see what suits you the best.

You may create a spreadsheet for tracking your finances that suits your needs and keeps you informed, in control, and organized by following these steps. Over time, make necessary adjustments and improvements to your spreadsheet to reflect changes in your goals or budget.

Selecting the appropriate spreadsheet program

Selecting the best spreadsheet program is essential to handling your money well. To assist you in making an informed choice, take into account the following:

Accessibility: Take into account how you'll open and utilize the spreadsheet program. Apple Numbers or Microsoft Excel can be good choices if you're a desktop app user. A well-liked option if you value cloud-based accessibility and teamwork is Google Sheets.

Make sure the spreadsheet program you use is compatible with the operating systems and devices you use. The majority of spreadsheet apps provide versions for Windows, macOS, iOS, and Android; however, it's crucial to confirm compatibility before choosing.

Functionality and Features: Consider the features and functionalities that each spreadsheet program has to offer. Look for features like pivot tables, conditional formatting, charts and graphs, formulas, and teamwork tools. Select financial management software that provides the necessary features for efficient financial management.

Ease of Use: Take into account the spreadsheet software's user interface and usability. Especially if you're new to spreadsheet apps, choose software that you find intuitive and user-friendly as some programs may have a steeper learning curve than others.

Integration: Find out if the spreadsheet program is compatible with the other programs and services you use. For instance, Google Sheets interfaces with Google Drive and other Google Workspace technologies, while Microsoft Excel easily connects with other Microsoft Office programs.

Cost: Take into account your financial restrictions and compare the prices of each spreadsheet program. While some apps, like Microsoft Excel, could need a membership or one-time payment, others, like Google Sheets, offer free versions with restricted functionality.

Collaboration: Software with strong collaboration features should be given top priority if you intend to work with others on your financial spreadsheets. To make teamwork and communication more efficient, look for features like real-time editing, commenting, and sharing.

Security: Verify that data security and privacy are given top priority in the spreadsheet program you select. To guard against illegal access or security lapses, look for features like encryption, access limits, and secure cloud storage.

Support and Documentation: Take into account whether the spreadsheet software has access to support and documentation. Seek out resources to aid in your understanding of the product and debugging any issues, such as tutorials, help guides, forums, and customer service channels.

Assess the extent and level of activity of the user base and the environment that surrounds the spreadsheet program. You can get helpful advice, tools, and support from a thriving community to make the most out of the software you use to manage your finances.

In the end, your unique needs, tastes, and workflow will determine which spreadsheet program is best for you. To select the program that best meets your needs and aids in efficient money management, take the time to investigate and contrast several choices.

CHAPTER TWO

Monitoring Revenue

A crucial component of successfully managing your finances is keeping track of your income. Whether you receive a single paycheck or several, being able to budget, plan for costs, and track your financial development is made possible by maintaining precise records of your earnings. Here's how to properly monitor income:

List All of Your Sources of Income: To begin, list all of your sources of income. This could include any regular income you receive, such as dividends from investments, salaries, wages, bonuses, freelancing, rental income, and other income. Make sure you thoroughly record every source of revenue.

Make Income groups: To add organization and clarity, group your income into appropriate groups. Typical income ranges could be:

Pay/Salary

Contract/Freelance Work

Income from Investments

Rental Revenue

Side Business Revenues

Other Income

Select a Tracking Technique: Choose the tracking technique that you find most effective.

A spreadsheet, financial software, budgeting applications, or even just a pen and paper can be used. Pick a system that works for you, one that makes it simple for you to enter and organize your revenue.

Make it a practice to promptly report revenue as soon as it is received. This gives you a current and accurate picture of your financial status and guarantees that your records are accurate. Schedule time on a regular basis to add new revenue transactions to your tracking database.

Be Specific: List every income transaction in full, including the amount received, the date it was received, the source of the money, and any pertinent memos or notes. This degree of specificity gives you important insights into your earning patterns and makes it easier for you to track your money.

Keep Track of Frequency: Make a note of how often each source of revenue occurs—weekly, biweekly, monthly, or irregularly. It is easier to budget for costs and better manage cash flow when you are aware of when your revenue is coming in.

Keep an eye out for Variability: Recognize any variations or peaks in your sources of revenue. While some sources of income could be steady and regular, others might change every month. Recognizing the fluctuations in your earnings enables you to make appropriate plans and budgets.

Reconcile Often: To guarantee accuracy and spot inconsistencies, reconcile your income data on a regular basis. To ensure that all revenue has been accurately recorded, compare your tracked income with pay stubs, bank statements, and other financial records.

Automate if You Can: To save time and minimize human labor, think about automating the income monitoring process wherever you can. Numerous budgeting and financial applications come with capabilities that classify your revenue transactions for you and sync automatically with your bank accounts.

examine and evaluate: To obtain knowledge of your earning trends, spot areas for improvement, and make wise financial decisions, examine and evaluate your income data on a regular basis. Make use of your income tracking data to guide your investing strategy, savings objectives, and budgeting.

You may make well-informed decisions and reach your financial objectives by keeping a systematic and continuous track of your income. This will provide you a clear picture of your financial status. Accurate income tracking is essential to sound financial management, regardless of your goals paying off debt, building long-term wealth, or saving for a big purchase.

Accounting for Expenses

Keeping track of your spending is essential to good money management. It enables you to track where your money is going, see trends in your spending, and make wise choices to reach your financial objectives. Here's how to properly report your expenses:

Keep Track of All Expenses: No matter how minor the expense, begin by recording it. This covers both variable and constant costs, such as groceries, eating out, transportation, utilities, entertainment, and luxuries. Examples of fixed expenses are rent or mortgage payments. Make sure to accurately document every expense.

Sort Expenses: To give your spending structure and clarity, sort them into different categories. Typical cost categories could be:

Housing (utilities, property taxes, rent or mortgage)

Public transportation, petrol, and auto payments

Food (restaurants, groceries)

Wellness and Health (medical treatment, insurance costs, gym memberships)

Toiletries and haircuts for personal hygiene

amusement (films, live performances, and streaming services)

Payments for debt (school loans, credit card debt)

Investments and Savings

Unrelated Expenses

Select a Tracking Technique: Choose the tracking technique that you find most effective. A spreadsheet, financial software, budgeting tools, or even a specific smartphone app for tracking expenses can all be used. Pick a system that works for you, one that makes it simple for you to enter and arrange your spending.

Keep Accurate Records: Develop the practice of keeping accurate records of your spending as they happen. This gives you a current and precise picture of your spending patterns and guarantees that your records are correct. Allocate a consistent period of time to enter fresh expenditure transactions into your monitoring platform.

Be Specific: List every spending transaction in full, including the date, the vendor or merchant, the category, the amount, and any pertinent memoranda or notes. This degree of specificity gives you important insights into your spending habits and makes it easier for you to keep track of your costs.

Keep Track of Payment Method: Whether it's cash, debit card, credit card, or electronic transfer, make a note of the payment method used for each expense. It's easier to control cash flow and keep an eye on your finances when you know how you're paying for things.

Watch Your Spending Trends: Over time, keep an eye on your spending patterns to spot areas where you might be overspending or where you might be able to make some savings. Examine your spending habits for trends and variances, then make the necessary adjustments to your budget.

Set Budget Limits: Based on your priorities and financial goals, set budget limits for every area of spending. Establish reasonable spending goals and monitor your progress toward sticking to your budget by using your documented expenses as a guide.

Reconcile Often: To guarantee accuracy and spot inconsistencies, reconcile your spending data on a frequent basis. To ensure that every transaction has been accurately recorded, check your monitored spending against receipts, credit card statements, and bank statements.

Review and Analyze: Review and analyze your expenditure data on a regular basis to learn more about your spending patterns, spot areas where you may cut costs, and make wise financial decisions. Make use of your spending logs to prioritize your financial objectives, find areas for growth, and inform budgeting.

You can develop a thorough awareness of your spending patterns by keeping a systematic and continuous record of your expenses. This is crucial for managing your money well. Accurate cost monitoring is a vital component of financial management, regardless of your goals—paying off debt, saving for a big purchase, or accumulating long-term wealth.

Sorting Out Expenses

Organizing your spending into categories is essential to managing your money well. You can learn more about your spending patterns, spot potential areas of overspending, and make well-informed decisions to reach your financial objectives by classifying your expenses. Here's how to properly categorize your expenses:

Decide on Common Expense Categories: To begin, decide on common expense categories that correspond to your priorities and spending patterns. Typical categories consist of:

Housing (utilities, property taxes, rent or mortgage, upkeep)

Transportation (gas, auto insurance, public transportation, upkeep)

Food (restaurant, grocery, coffee, and snacks)

Wellness and Health (medical treatment, insurance costs, gym memberships, and prescription drugs)

Personal hygiene (hair cuts, makeup, toiletries)

Amusement (films, live performances, streaming services, pastimes)

Payments for debt (credit card, personal, and education loans)

Savings and Investments (investment accounts, emergency fund savings, retirement contributions)

Other costs (subscriptions, gifts, contributions, and pet care)

Customize Categories to Meet Your Needs: Adjust the spending categories to match your particular lifestyle and financial circumstances. To properly reflect your spending habits and priorities, think about creating or changing the categories. For greater specificity and complexity, you can also make subcategories inside of main categories.

Employ a Consistent System: To guarantee accuracy and consistency, create a consistent system for classifying spending. When recording spending, choose a set list of categories and subcategories and stick to it. This facilitates the tracking of spending patterns over time and the comparison of expenses between various time periods.

Group Similar Expenses Together: To make tracking easier, group similar expenses together within each category. For instance, you might have subcategories for shopping, eating out, and coffee/snacks under the "Food" category. You can find chances for savings and have a better understanding of where your money is going by grouping related items together.

Be Particular and Detailed: To properly classify an expense transaction, provide comprehensive details on each one. Add the amount, category, merchant/vendor, date, and any pertinent memos or notes. Your expense records will be thorough and educational if you are specific and detailed.

Review and Update Categories Frequently: Make sure your spending categories appropriately represent your priorities and current financial status by reviewing them frequently. You might need to add, edit, or remove categories as your spending patterns change or develop in order to best suit your needs.

Prioritize Essential vs. Discretionary Expenses: Within your categories, make a distinction between essential expenses (such housing, utilities, and groceries) and discretionary expenses (like eating out and entertainment). This assists you in setting spending priorities and choosing wisely where to spend your money.

Employ Apps or Software with predetermined Categories: Take into account utilizing budgeting applications or financial software that provides predetermined categories for expenses. While offering a predetermined list of popular categories to select from, many apps let you modify categories according to your tastes. In the process of configuring your expense tracking system, this can save time and work.

You may better understand your spending patterns, spot areas for savings, and make well-informed decisions to reach your financial objectives by properly classifying your expenses. Establish a thorough and well-organized system for classifying your spending, and make sure it is updated and reviewed on a regular basis to keep it current and aligned with your priorities.

Planning and Observation

Effective financial management requires both monitoring and budgeting. Making a strategy for how you will divide your income to pay bills, save money, and reach your financial objectives is known as budgeting. Monitoring is keeping tabs on your earnings, outlays, and advancement toward your set financial goals. Here's how to successfully manage your finances and create a budget:

Set Financial Objectives: To begin, decide on specific financial objectives. These could be debt repayment, emergency fund building, housing down payment savings, or retirement investment. Your objectives will direct your efforts in monitoring and budgeting.

Compute Your Income: Find out how much money you make each month overall from all sources, such as rent, freelance work, bonuses, salaries, and wages. Use your net income (after taxes and deductions) to get a true sense of how much money you have available.

Determine Fixed and Variable Expenses: Distinguish between fixed expenses, which are monthly costs that are essentially the same, like rent or a mortgage, utilities, and insurance premiums, and variable expenses, which are monthly costs that vary, like groceries, eating out, and entertainment.

Establish a Budget: Make sure you are living within your means by allocating your income to meet your debt obligations, savings objectives, and expenses. Choose a budgeting strategy that works best for you, such as zero-based budgeting (where every dollar is allocated to a specific area) or the 50/30/20 rule (which states that 50% of income should be used for needs, 30% for wants, and 20% for savings or debt repayment).

Keep Track of Your Expenses: Make a note of every item you incur and arrange them into the appropriate budget categories. You have two options for doing this: automatically link your accounts to a budgeting tool that classifies transactions for you, or do it manually using a spreadsheet, financial software, or budgeting applications.

Monitor Your expenditure: To make sure you're remaining on track, compare your expenditure on a regular basis to your allocated targets. Track your progress toward your financial objectives and make necessary adjustments to your budget to account for variations in your income or out-of-pocket spending.

Modify as Needed: Remain adaptable and prepared to make changes to your budget when needed. Look for methods to reduce your spending or reallocate money if you discover that you're routinely going over budget in several areas. In a similar vein, think about modifying your budget to account for any windfall or drop in spending.

Review Frequently: Make time each month to go over your spending plan and budget. Examine your spending habits, note any areas that need work, and acknowledge any advancements made toward your financial objectives. Reviewing frequently enables you to stay focused on your long-term goals and make necessary course corrections.

To maintain your motivation and commitment to your budgeting and monitoring efforts, prioritize your financial goals. Envision the advantages of accomplishing your objectives and remind yourself of the strides you've already achieved.

Seek Assistance if Needed: Don't be afraid to ask a financial expert, counselor, or dependable friend or family member for assistance if you're having trouble making or adhering to a budget. They can assist you in achieving financial success by offering direction, accountability, and support.

You can take charge of your finances, lessen financial stress, and work toward your long-term financial objectives by creating an effective budget and keeping an eye on your spending. To lay a strong foundation for a safe and prosperous future, incorporate budgeting and monitoring into your daily financial practice.

CHAPTER THREE

Establishing a budget based on earnings and outlays

A vital first step in practicing sound financial management is creating a budget based on your income and expenses. This is how to make a budget that supports your goals and your financial reality:

Compute Your Monthly Income: To begin, figure out how much money you make each month overall. This covers all forms of income, including commissions, revenues from freelancing, bonuses, salaries, wages, and any other type of revenue. To accurately determine the amount of money you have available, use your net income (after taxes and deductions).

Make a thorough record of all the money you spend each month by creating an expenditure list. Make a distinction between variable and fixed expenses. Variable expenses are those that change from month to month and include groceries, eating out, entertainment, and rent or mortgage, utilities, and insurance payments.

Sort Your costs: To give structure and clarity, sort your costs into different categories. Typical categories include debt repayment, savings, food, housing, transportation, healthcare, and discretionary spending. For further in-depth tracking, you can further divide these categories into subcategories.

Assign Dollar Amounts to Each Category: Compute an approximate monthly expenditure for each category of expenses. To calculate average expenditure amounts, consult previous bank statements, credit card statements, and receipts. When making estimates, be sure to take seasonal or erratic expenses into consideration.

Compute Your Total spending: To find your total monthly spending, add up the projected amounts for each category of expenses. This provides you with a starting point for calculating the amount of money you'll need to pay for all of your bills and personal expenses.

Subtract Expenses from Income: Make a comparison between your monthly income and expenses. The ideal situation would be for your income to be higher than your costs, giving you extra money to put toward debt repayment, savings, or other financial objectives. You will need to make adjustments to your budget in order to balance it if your spending are higher than your income.

Allocate Money Wisely: Set spending priorities by dividing up your budget into categories of expenditure according to your priorities and financial objectives. After covering necessities like housing, utilities, and groceries, divide the remaining money among categories of discretionary spending.

Review and Adjust Often: To keep track of your actual expenditure versus your planned amounts, review your budget on a regular basis. Whenever your income, expenses, or financial objectives change, make the necessary adjustments to your budget. To make sure your budget stays reasonable and reachable, be adaptable and prepared to make adjustments.

Set aside money for savings objectives, such as accumulating an emergency fund, putting money down for a down payment on a house, or making retirement investments. Make savings a priority in your budget and see them as an expense that cannot be avoided.

Monitor Your Progress: By often examining your budget and keeping tabs on your expenditures, you can keep track of how well you're doing financially. Celebrate your progress and accomplishments, and take any setbacks as an opportunity to improve your budgeting technique.

By making a budget based on your income and expenses, you can take control of your money, reduce financial stress, and work toward both short- and long-term financial goals. To lay a strong basis for financial success, incorporate budgeting into your daily financial routine.

Making Reports and Visualizations

Your spending patterns, savings progress, and general financial health can all be better understood by building reports and visualizations using your budget and financial data. Here's how to make reports and visualizations to aid in your improved understanding and management of your finances:

Pick the Correct Tools: To begin, decide which tools are best for producing reports and visualizations. Spreadsheet programs like Google Sheets and Microsoft Excel are common choices, as are specialized data visualization programs like Tableau, Power BI, or Google Data Studio. Select a tool that has the capabilities you require and is appropriate for your level of expertise.

Organize Your Data: Make sure the structure and organization of your financial data make it simple to examine and visualize. To organize your spreadsheet's revenue, expenses, savings, and other financial transactions, use different sheets or tabs. Make sure all of the data points have consistent, legible labels.

Select Crucial measurements: Choose the crucial measurements and perspectives that you wish to illustrate and present. This could include overall revenue, overall spending, savings rate, category-specific spending, debt payback progress, investment performance, and more. Determine which metrics are most pertinent to your financial objectives and aspirations.

Choose Visualization Types: To effectively depict your data, choose the visualization types that are most relevant. Typical forms of visualization are as follows:

Bar charts: Analyze values from various time periods or categories.

Display patterns and trends over time with line charts.

Pie charts: Show how something is made up overall (e.g., expenses by category).

Emphasize cumulative totals throughout time using area charts.

Examine the connections between two variables using scatter plots.

Heatmaps: Show patterns or data density.

Make visuals: Based on your financial data, make visuals using the tool of your choice. Begin by deciding on the right data range and the sort of visualization that best captures the insights you wish to share. To make your visualizations more comprehensible and visually appealing, add titles, labels, colors, and other formatting options.

Examine Trends & Patterns: Examine the visuals to find patterns, trends, and oddities in your financial information. Throughout time, keep an eye out for instances where you might be overspending, chances to save money, or shifts in your financial habits. Make use of the newfound knowledge to guide your financial planning and budgeting decisions.

Generate Summaries: Assemble your data into concise reports that offer a thorough synopsis of your financial condition. Incorporate important indicators, patterns, and useful information to assist you in making financially-wise decisions. To monitor your financial goals' advancement, think about generating reports on a monthly, quarterly, or annual basis.

Share and Cooperate: To get more viewpoints and comments, show your reports and visualizations to family members, close friends, or financial experts. Work together to pinpoint areas that require improvement and create plans for accomplishing your financial goals.

Review and Update Often: To reflect changes in your financial condition or goals, review and update your reports and visualizations on a regular basis. Allocate a certain period of time every month or quarter to examine your financial information, refresh your charts, and make any necessary modifications to your spending plan.

Monitor Your Progress: Utilize reports and infographics to monitor your advancement over time toward your financial objectives. Keep an eye on important indicators and benchmarks, acknowledge successes, and modify your plan as needed to keep on course to meet your goals.

You can obtain important insights into your financial habits, spot areas for improvement, and make well-informed decisions to reach your financial objectives by building visualizations and reports based on your budget and financial data. By using this type of financial visualization, you may maintain your motivation, accountability, and focus while working for a stable financial future.

Creating graphs and charts to illustrate financial data

Creating graphs and charts to display financial data can give you important information about your general financial health, savings status, and spending patterns. Here's how to create graphs and charts to efficiently visualize your financial data:

Pick the Correct program: Opt for a program or piece of software that makes it simple for you to make charts and graphs. Spreadsheet programs like Google Sheets and Microsoft Excel are common choices, as are specialized data visualization programs like Tableau, Power BI, or Google Data Studio. Choose a tool that has the functionality you require and is appropriate for your level of expertise.

Organize Your Financial Data: Make sure the structure and organization of your financial data make it simple to examine and display. To show distinct data categories, such as income, expenses, savings, and debt, use separate columns or rows. Give each data point a consistent and obvious label.

Choose Important Metrics: Choose the important metrics and insights that you wish to display. This could include overall revenue, overall spending, savings rate, category-specific spending, debt payback progress, investment performance, and more. Determine which metrics are most pertinent to your financial objectives and aspirations.

Choose the Correct Chart Types: To successfully depict your financial data, choose the right chart types. Typical chart types used to illustrate financial data are as follows:

Bar charts: Analyze values from various time periods or categories.

Display patterns and trends over time with line charts.

Pie charts: Show how something is made up overall (e.g., expenses by category).

Emphasize cumulative totals throughout time using area charts.

Examine the connections between two variables using scatter plots.

Heatmaps: Show patterns or data density.

Make Charts and Graphs: Based on your financial data, make charts and graphs using the tool of your choice. First, decide which chart format best conveys the insights you want to provide and what data range is appropriate. To make your charts more comprehensible and visually appealing, add titles, labels, colors, and other formatting options.

Examine Trends and Patterns: Examine the graphs and charts for any abnormalities, trends, or patterns in your financial data. Throughout time, keep an eye out for instances where you might be overspending, chances to save money, or shifts in your financial habits. Make use of the newfound knowledge to guide your financial planning and budgeting decisions.

Combine Multiple Charts: To give a thorough perspective of your financial status, think about integrating multiple charts and graphs into a single dashboard or report. This enables you to visualize the relationships between various areas of your money and compare them using different measures.

Add Contextual Information: To aid in the effective interpretation of the charts and graphs, include contextual information and annotations. To give the data visualizations context and clarity, add titles, labels, legends, and explanatory notes.

Share and Cooperate: To get more viewpoints and comments, show your charts and graphs to family members, close friends, or financial experts. Work together to pinpoint areas that require improvement and create plans for accomplishing your financial goals.

check and Update Often: To reflect changes in your financial condition or goals, check and update your charts and graphs on a regular basis. Allocate a certain period of time every month or quarter to examine your financial information, refresh your charts, and make any necessary modifications to your spending plan.

You may track your progress toward your goals, obtain important insights into your financial habits, and make well-informed decisions to improve your financial well-being by using charts and graphs to represent your financial data. This kind of financial visualization can support you in reaching your financial goals by keeping you accountable, motivated, and focused.

Streamlining and Automating Procedures

Process simplification and automation in financial management can increase productivity, decrease errors, and save time. Here's how to simplify and automate procedures to make money management easier:

Establish Automatic Payments: Set up automatic payments for loans, utilities, bills, and other recurring costs. The majority of banks provide online bill payment services that let you plan payments ahead of time and guarantee that bills are paid automatically on time.

Utilize Mobile Apps and Online Banking: Manage your accounts, send money, deposit checks, and keep an eye on transactions all from anywhere with the help of mobile apps and online banking. To make banking operations easier for you and keep you informed about your finances, several banks offer tools like account alerts and mobile check deposit.

Establish Direct Deposit: Make arrangements for your paychecks and other sources of money to be deposited directly into your bank account. The use of paper checks and manual depositing is eliminated with direct deposit, guaranteeing prompt and safe access to funds.

Automate Contributions to Savings Accounts: Establish regular, automatic payments from your checking account to your investment or savings accounts. By continually contributing to your savings, this "pay yourself first" strategy will help you meet your financial objectives more quickly.

Use Budgeting applications and Software: Make use of budgeting applications and software to automatically track your spending, establish budgets, and keep an eye on your financial situation. These programs frequently classify transactions, link with your credit cards and bank accounts, and offer real-time insights into your spending patterns.

Employ Expense Tracking software: To automatically classify expenditures, track expenses, and gather receipts, make use of expense tracking software. You may take pictures of your receipts and have the necessary information automatically extracted for tax and expense reporting purposes with apps like Receipt Bank and Expensify.

Set Up Alerts and Notifications: To keep track of account activity, low balances, odd transactions, and impending payments, enable alerts and notifications from your bank or other financial organizations. Alerts can assist you in seeing any problems early and acting quickly to resolve them.

Consolidate Accounts and Services: By combining loans, investments, and accounts with fewer organizations, you can streamline your financial accounts and services. Consolidation can lessen paperwork, streamline account management, and facilitate tracking your whole financial picture.

Automate Debt Repayment: To guarantee that your minimum monthly payments are made on time, set up automated payments if you have credit card or loan debt. To reduce interest costs and pay off debt sooner, think about raising payments or establishing expedited repayment programs.

Review and Optimize Frequently: Make sure your automated processes are operating as intended by reviewing them frequently and making necessary adjustments. To stay on track and make modifications as your financial situation changes, keep a close eye on your accounts, budget, and savings targets on a regular basis.

You can gain more control over your funds, save time, and lessen stress by automating and optimizing procedures in your financial management. Utilize automation tools and technology to streamline processes, increase productivity, and concentrate your time and efforts on reaching your financial objectives.

Configuring recurrent payments for consistent outlays

One easy strategy to guarantee that invoices are paid on time and avoid manual involvement is to set up recurring transactions for frequent costs. To set up recurring transactions for your normal expenses, follow these steps:

Determine Recurring Expenses: Create a list of all the regular expenses that you incur on a regular basis, such as utilities, insurance premiums, rent or mortgage payments, subscriptions, loan payments, and memberships.

Select Payment form: Choose the form of payment that you will apply to each recurrent expense. You can use a credit or debit card, set up automatic payments straight from your bank account, or plan payments using your bank's online bill pay services.

Set Up Automatic Payments with Vendors: Get in touch with the vendor or service provider to arrange automatic payments for expenses that are fixed each month, like rent or loan payments. Give the seller permission to debit your account on the agreed-upon date by giving them your bank account or credit card information, indicating the amount and frequency of payments.

Use Online Bill Pay Services: You can set up recurring payments for bills and costs by using the online bill pay services that are offered by many banks. To set up recurring payments, go into your online banking account, go to the bill pay section, and follow the instructions. For every recurring transaction, you may set the start date, frequency, payee, and payment amount.

Plan Your Payments: Determine the frequency and timing of each recurring transaction by taking into account your billing cycle and the dates of due. Decide if you want payments to be made every week, every two weeks, every month, or at a different period. You can also choose when the recurring payments will begin.

Monitor and Review: Make sure your recurring transactions are being processed promptly and accurately by regularly reviewing them. Recurring payment setups may be impacted by changes to your costs or billing information, so be sure to keep note of payment dates, amounts, and any changes.

Modify as Needed: If your financial circumstances change, be ready to modify your periodic transactions. Update your payment details with suppliers and service providers if you change banks. Similar to this, to prevent incurring extra fees, when you quit a membership or subscription, don't forget to stop the associated recurring payment.

Think About Using Apps for Budgeting: A few of these apps have features that let you keep track of regular spending and set up automatic payments right from the app. Check to see if the software you like best for budgeting has this feature, then make use of it to simplify your money handling.

Account Balances: Make sure you have enough money in your bank accounts to pay for your regular costs by keeping a watch on your balances. Prior to the processing of planned payments, set up alerts or notifications from your bank to inform you of low balances or insufficient money.

Review Frequently: Evaluate your recurring transactions on a regular basis to determine their necessity and applicability. To free up money for other priorities, stop making any recurring payments for any services or subscriptions you no longer need or use.

CHAPTER FOUR

You may automate bill payments, avert late fees, and make sure that your financial commitments are fulfilled on time each month by setting up recurring transactions for your usual spending. Utilize bill-paying services, budgeting software, and online banking tools to streamline the process and maintain financial control.

Protecting and Backing Up Your Spreadsheet

To guard against loss, theft, or illegal access to your financial data, you must secure and back up your spreadsheet. Here's how to successfully backup and secure your spreadsheet:

Create a habit of routinely saving backups of your spreadsheet to guard against data loss in the event of file corruption, unintentional deletion, or other unanticipated circumstances. Back up your data to a cloud storage provider, USB flash drive, external hard drive, or other safe place.

Utilize Version Control: To keep track of changes and roll back to earlier versions as necessary, take advantage of the version control features found in some spreadsheet programs and cloud-based platforms. Version control makes sure you can simply recover from mistakes or errors and maintain access to historical data.

Encrypt Sensitive Data: To avoid unwanted access, think about encrypting any spreadsheet that includes sensitive financial data, such as account numbers, passwords, or personally identifiable information. For added security, password-protect sensitive spreadsheet sheets or use encryption software.

Secure Access Controls: Grant only authorized people access to your spreadsheet. Configure permissions and access restrictions in the spreadsheet program or cloud storage service to limit who can access, edit, or download the file. For extra security, set up two-factor authentication and create strong, one-of-a-kind passwords.

Install and update antivirus and antimalware software on your computer to guard against malware, viruses, and other security risks that could jeopardize your bank information or spreadsheet. To prevent malware infestations, exercise caution when downloading files or opening attachments from unidentified sources.

Update Software Frequently: Stay current on security patches and upgrades for your operating system, spreadsheet program, and security software. Updates for software frequently include patches for security holes and known vulnerabilities that an attacker could use against you.

Watch Account behavior: Keep a watch on your finances and accounts for any unusual behavior that might point to fraud or illegal access. Regularly check your bank and credit card statements, and notify your financial institution right away of any inconsistencies or unauthorized expenditures.

Safe Physical Access: If you save spreadsheet backups on physical media, like USB flash drives or external hard drives, make sure they are kept out of the reach of unauthorized individuals and in a secure place. For added security against loss or theft, think about utilizing a secured cabinet or safe.

Educate Others and Yourself: Keep up to date on the latest cybersecurity dangers and safest methods for protecting your personal financial information. Teach those who have access to the spreadsheet and yourself the value of cybersecurity as well as how to spot and steer clear of malware, phishing frauds, and other online hazards.

Create a plan for data recovery in the event of an emergency, such as a security breach or data loss. Determine the steps for restoring data from backups, how to contact IT support, and backup protocols in order to reduce downtime and lessen the effects of security incidents.

You can safeguard the integrity and security of your financial data and prevent loss, theft, or unwanted access by properly backing up and safeguarding your spreadsheet. To reduce threats and ensure your financial well-being, take proactive measures to secure your spreadsheet and adhere to cybersecurity best practices.

Saving your spreadsheet often and keeping backup copies

It is essential to regularly save your spreadsheet and keep backup copies in order to guard against data loss and guarantee the accuracy of your financial data. Here's how to backup and save your spreadsheet efficiently:

Configure Automatic Saving: The majority of spreadsheet programs, including Google Sheets and Microsoft Excel, offer automatic saving options. By turning on this function, you can lower the chance of losing data in the event of a software crash or power loss by having your spreadsheet automatically store changes at predetermined intervals.

Manually Save Changes: Make it a habit to manually save your spreadsheet on a frequent basis in addition to automatically saving it, particularly after making big updates or changes. To save the most recent version of your file, use the "Save" or "Save As" feature of your spreadsheet program.

Utilize Version Control: To keep track of modifications and manage several versions of your spreadsheet, take into consideration utilizing the version control tools found in certain spreadsheet programs and cloud-based platforms. Version control preserves a history of all modifications made over time and lets you roll back to earlier iterations as needed.

Make a backup copy of your spreadsheet and save it on external storage media, including USB flash drives, external hard drives, or network-attached storage (NAS) devices. Depending on your needs, set up a regular backup plan for your spreadsheet, such as weekly or monthly.

Utilize Cloud Storage: Store spreadsheet backups safely in the cloud by utilizing cloud storage services such as Microsoft OneDrive, Dropbox, and Google Drive. The benefit of cloud storage is that it can be accessed from any location with an internet connection and has built-in redundancy to prevent data loss.

Encrypt Backups: To prevent unwanted access to important financial data in your spreadsheet, think about encrypting backups. Before saving backup data to the cloud or external drive, encrypt them using the tools or capabilities your backup software offers.

Label and Arrange Backups: To make it simple to locate and access particular spreadsheet versions when needed, clearly label and arrange backup files. To keep backups accessible and organized, use descriptive folder names and file names.

Test Backups Frequently: Make sure your backup files can be successfully opened and restored in the event of data loss or corruption by testing them frequently. Periodically do test restores to ensure the integrity of your backups and make any required modifications to your backup plan.

Store Backups Offsite: You should think about keeping backup copies of your spreadsheet in a safe place offsite to guard against physical harm or the loss of your primary storage location. For offsite backups, use a safe deposit box, a trusted friend's or relative's house, or a secure cloud storage service.

Evaluate and Update Backup Strategy: To make sure your backup plan is still efficient and meets your needs, evaluate and update it on a regular basis. As your spreadsheet, storage technology, or security requirements change, make the necessary updates.

Your spreadsheet can be periodically saved, backups kept, and data loss reduced to keep your financial information safe and easily available when needed. To safeguard your important financial data, put in place a thorough backup plan that include regular backups to external storage or the cloud, automatic and manual saving, and both.

Some Advice for Efficient Money Monitoring

To manage your money, gain insight into your spending patterns, and achieve your financial objectives, you must engage in effective financial tracking. Here are some pointers to assist you in efficiently managing your finances:

Make a Budget: To begin, make a budget that details your earnings, outlays, savings targets, and loan payback commitments. A budget guarantees that you manage your resources effectively and offers a structure for monitoring your financial behavior.

Employ a Tracking System: Whether it's a spreadsheet, an app for budgeting, or financial management software, pick a tracking system that suits your needs. Choose a system that is user-friendly, readily available, and equipped with the capabilities you require to efficiently monitor your earnings and outlays.

Make it a practice to keep track of all of your financial transactions, including your income, outlays, transfers, and investments. Track all of your transactions, big and little, to obtain a complete picture of your financial life.

Sort Your spending: To gain a better understanding of where your money is going, sort your spending into different categories. Housing, transportation, food, utilities, entertainment, and savings are some of common expense categories. Organizing your spending into categories enables you to spot potential areas of overspending and adapt as necessary.

Track Your Spending in Real-Time: Try to keep track of your expenditures as closely to real-time as you can. Utilize online banking resources or mobile apps to track and classify transactions as they happen. This assists you in managing your money and preventing unpleasant shocks at the end of the month.

Evaluate Frequently: Allocate a certain period of time every week or month to examine your financial dealings and evaluate your advancement toward your spending plan and financial objectives. Conducting routine evaluations enables you to spot any anomalies, monitor your expenditure trends, and make any corrections.

Tracking Should Be Automated: To make tracking easier, make use of automation tools and features. To save time and effort, set up recurring expense reminders, warnings for suspicious spending activity, and automatic transaction categorization.

Reconcile Accounts: Make sure that the recorded transactions in your accounts correspond to the real activity in them by routinely reconciling your bank statements, credit card statements, and other financial statements. Error detection, fraud detection, and precise record-keeping of finances are all aided by reconciliation.

Follow Your Debt Repayment Progress: If you have unpaid debt, keep track of your repayment progress to see how much you've paid down and how much is still owing. To see your progress and maintain motivation to pay off your debt, use debt payoff calculators or tracking software.

Remain Adaptable and Flexible: As your financial circumstances or aspirations change, be prepared to modify your budget and tracking strategies accordingly. As life events, costs, and income fluctuate, modify your tracking strategy as necessary to maintain your progress toward your financial goals.

You can take charge of your finances, make wise decisions, and strive toward your financial objectives by using these helpful financial monitoring ideas. Building a solid basis for a safe financial future can be facilitated by maintaining accurate and consistent tracking, which is essential for financial success.

Reliability and precision in transaction documentation

For efficient financial tracking and administration, transaction recording must be accurate and consistent. The following advice can help you make sure that your financial transactions are consistently and accurately recorded:

Create a habit: Assign designated periods each day or week to update your financial records. This will help you establish a habit for recording transactions. Maintaining accurate financial data and preventing missing transactions require consistency.

Use One recording Method: Whether it's a spreadsheet, financial management software, or an app for budgeting, decide on a single approach or tool for recording transactions. Using several approaches may cause misunderstandings and discrepancies in your documentation.

Document Transactions Promptly: Develop the habit of documenting transactions as soon as they happen, preferably the same day. This lowers the possibility that you will misremember transactions or make mistakes when you try to recall them later.

Be Specific and Detailed: Give every transaction specific details, such as the date, amount, payee, category, and any pertinent notes. You may more properly classify expenses and gain insight into your spending patterns by being specific.

Save Receipts and documents: When tracking expenses, refer to the receipts, invoices, and other supporting documents for your transactions. This guarantees correctness and offers proof in the event of audits or discrepancies.

Examine and Confirm Transactions: Make sure that the transactions you have recorded are accurate by periodically going over your financial records. To make sure there is consistency, check your records against bank statements, credit card statements, and other financial information.

Reconcile Accounts: Keep track of your recorded transactions and the real activity in your accounts by periodically reconciling your bank, credit card, and other financial accounts. Finding mistakes, duplicates, or missing transactions is aided by reconciliation.

Utilize Automation Tools: To expedite transaction recording and minimize manual data entry, make use of automation tools and features. Automated transaction importation and classification are provided by numerous financial management apps and budgeting apps.

Remain Organized: Ensure that your financial documents are readily available and arranged. To keep track of documents and records pertaining to your transactions, use digital filing systems, labels, or folders.

Train and Educate: Make sure that everyone involved in recording transactions receives the necessary instruction and training regarding the recording procedure and rules. Keeping accurate financial records requires consistency in both standards and recording methods.

These pointers can help you record transactions consistently and accurately, which is necessary for efficient budgeting, financial tracking, and decision-making. Maintaining accurate and consistent records will help you stay on track to meet your financial objectives by giving you a clear picture of your current financial status.

CONCLUSION

In summary, using a spreadsheet to total your money has a lot of advantages and gives you a complete tool for efficiently managing your financial information. You may track your income, expenses, savings, assets, and obligations in one place by making use of spreadsheet software. This makes it possible for you to organize, analyze, and decide on your financial status more effectively.

You can tailor your approach to financial management to your unique needs and objectives by putting in place a spreadsheet-based financial tracking system. In your financial management endeavors, a well-crafted spreadsheet may be an invaluable tool for tracking monthly spending, keeping tabs on savings growth, and evaluating investment success.

Additionally, you may modify your financial tracking system over time as your goals and circumstances change thanks to the scalability and flexibility of spreadsheet software. To improve productivity and accuracy, you can add new features, automate some tasks, or improve your tracking techniques.

Spreadsheets are a great tool for financial management, but in order to guarantee accuracy and dependability, they also need to be used carefully and maintained on a regular basis. Updating and error-free financial data requires regular updates, reconciliations, and checks.

In conclusion, you gain more control and understanding of your financial situation when you use a spreadsheet to keep track of your finances. You may make wise decisions, monitor your progress toward your objectives, and eventually attain more financial stability and security by utilizing the features of spreadsheet software and good financial tracking techniques.

THE END

www.ingramcontent.com/pod-product-compliance
Lightning Source LLC
Chambersburg PA
CBHW060430290526
45791CB00002B/916